A Peace of Lovelace

Tamisha Binion

A Peace of Lovelace

Editor:Mai Xiong
Format: Silvie Drouillard of Elijah Jean Editing
Illustration: Jaraud Lotice Lott
Cover Photographer: Nahara Studios Photographer Naseer Clemmer

ISBN -13: 978-0-578-46512-8

For more information contact:
tamishab.012@gmail.com

Facebook: Peace.of.Lovelace
Twitter: PeaceOfLovelace
Instagram:Peace.of.Lovelace

DEDICATION

My Son, My Sun

My Son, my Sun. I don't know where to start...I could write a book on how you got my whole heart. You are the son of God; you're my life.I would go to war for you with blood dripping from my hands. You're the messiah, it's only right.

CONTENTS

INTRODUCTION

Within your soul there are doors that lead to unspoken emotions, things that you are ashamed to admit, and a flesh that is trying to overpower your spirit. These are doors that you closed and never wanted to step foot in again. "A PEACE of Lovelace" will be the key for you to willingly open those doors. Now you're asking why should I opened these doors if they're closed for a reason? You walk pass these doors everyday knowing one day you need to open it; to get serenity in your life. Well today is that day! Rebuild a piece of your soul with peace and reconcile with oneself.

The book is entitled "A PEACE of Lovelace" Peace defining both meanings piece and peace. The name Lovelace is my great grandmother's maiden name. I have carried the name Lovelace as a nickname. I chose this title because I'll be giving you a PIECE of me, Lovelace. Documenting my feelings, thoughts, strengths, weaknesses, and my heart all in my poems. Bring you PEACE through me by highlighting some of the most memorable moments of my life, good and bad. Embark on my journey to accepting apologies that was never giving, self-forgiveness, self-love, self-healing, and self-discovery. This book will help you understand that love also means to let go and there's beauty with letting go because where there is an ending there is a beginning. Learning to accept there's some situations you can't control. The universe controls time. It brings you people and takes you places at the moment it chooses to, right or wrong.

God's Child

I want true love, just not your type of love.
I want true love, the kind that God put in me.
I don't want to leave this earth without meeting you,
God's child, and God's son.
I want to feel God in you, but sometimes what you show me isn't
God's love.
Do I wait for you just like God has made many men do? Or, do I
leave?
The thing is, I see good in you; peace, love, and happiness letting me
know God is somewhere in you.
Now you should understand, but the problem is that you need to see
it too. That true love that God put in you.

Mind of A Queen

Her greatest asset isn't her ass, but her mind.
You're so focused on her appearance you don't even
see the beauty on the inside.
She has a mind that is one of a kind.
Filled with goals, morals, and pure greatness.
Be cautious when you approach her, she may just be too dope for
you.

7 Years

Some days, I feel like I wasted 7 years of my life with you.
You hit me with that, "I'm not ready for what you're ready for."
If you knew that shit, why didn't you let me go? I put my heart and
soul into loving you. I can't put all the blame on you because I
allowed myself to put up with you.
The day I knew I had to let you go, I'm happy I did. I found a piece
of myself that I forgot 7 years ago. So, it wasn't a waste of my time. It
was a journey to self-love and absolution.
I thank you for those 7 years

Lovelace I

All I want is closure, but you think I'm asking for too much.

Angel & Demon

She's innocent with a dirty mind.
At night she gets high and watches the shooting stars fly by.
In her dreams, she plays all night, but every morning arrives to work
on time.
Not big on going out but hits the streets sometimes.
She got hoes but never pay them any mind.
She's an angel with a little demon inside.

Her > Him

I just wanted you to hold me more.
We didn't love the same
I felt like I loved you a little more.

Cut Deep

I'm not worried if you love me or love me not.
What's not okay is when one's heart bleeds and takes forever to stop.
Like you really cut me deep.
I just want you to leave me be.
In tune with myself is where I'm trying to be.
Each day I'm patching my heart with peace, learning to have
patience, because I know these wounds are deep.

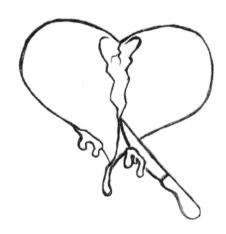

Control

Take control of the emotions that cannot be define.
In a loop of feelings that has no words behind it.
When you're honest with yourself about your weakness, your word
can be defined.

Right Wrong Time

Gray sweatpants.
wheat timbs.
long braids to the back.
chocolate skin.
Before you walked in I wished the rain would've washed away any sins
you were about to commit.
I met you at the right/wrong time in my life.
From that day forward, I encounter some of the most valuable lessons
in
life.

Lovelace II

You deserve better, so do better.
Carry your self-respect to the mountain top.

Kyrenia

Every morning you had fresh watermelon, cantaloupe, and toast on the table. You said, "Come and sit, let me talk to you."
You fed my mind and heart with your lovely wisdom and knowledge. You remind me to keep my evil eye close, to keep the negative energy away.
You told me, "Be free in the Mediterranean Sea, let the waves carry you away." You taught me to embrace my chinky eyes and the stretch marks on my thighs. Oh, how I miss that night we smoked hookah under the moonlight. From you, I learned to love myself with the natural beautiful things in life. You will forever have a special place in my heart Kyrenia

Peace with me

I fall in love with healing myself. I'm doing good now.
The level up was not to impress them but to improve me.
To give me peace.

Clowns And Merry Go Rounds

Is you going to protect me the way I do?
Maybe I'm being crazy or delusional to imagine you will console my
heart the way I do.
I'm be careful this time around, not jumping head first, but test the
water and looking around.
Feelings on a merry go around,
I'm ready to close this carnival down.

Sorry Not Sorry

Rise in every single aspect in life.
There will be people who may think you're disloyal just for wanting
better.
Don't apologize for evolving.

Different Type of Love

You're a part of me even though I don't want you to be.
Most times you can't even look me in the eyes.
Is it because there are some resentment?
We always meet to watch our seed grow.
Taking turns being the sun and the rain.
I grew with you. Somewhere in my heart there Is a spot for you.
Seeing your smile is bittersweet knowing you were a piece of me who
couldn't give me
peace

Lovelace III

At night these stretch marks turn into tiger stripes.

To You From Her

Dear Mister,

   I want to apologize in advance if I make it difficult for you to love me. It's just that I've been disrespected, neglected, and love another more than me. I don't want you to get the wrong impression. I'm not looking for sympathy, all I ever wanted was for someone to care for me. I pray your eyes don't paint this false illusion that will later make me cry and I pray you don't tell me savory lies. All I ask is that you be careful with me.

Sincerely,

Her

Heart of Dahomey

It's not a war that she began,
but it's a war she will end.
Sworn to protect the throne, which her heart resides on.
She knows the weak will never survive with all her emotions put to the
side.
She will fight to the death just to keep the heart alive.

5.21

You said,
"Know that no matter what situation life throws us, y'all will be my
No.1 priority!"
You lied to us.

Cold

My heart so cold.
Sometimes it feels like I got nothing to lose.
It's sad because I'm such a good person.
Does that make me the dangerous one?

Lesson Learned

She had a pure heart, but you didn't care for her right turning her colder than the winter night. You felt some type of way when she didn't say she missed you back. It would've been right if she did that. Knowing one day she won't get that love back from hurt. It's hard for her to trust again. Having to escape into a dark hole, just to get her mind right. Praying she would shine brightly before you came and dimmed her light. Putting her all into something that turned into nothing was just a lesson learned.

Exfoliate

Don't just exfoliate your skin but exfoliate your surroundings also.
It's people around that means you no good, but always wishing you
well.
They take joy in your downfalls. Let that dead layer go.

Queendom

A little insane.
Carmel brown skin.
Did I mention a little loco in the brain?
Sweetest girl in the world with a crowned made of golden curls.
Coconut oil dripping from her full lips.
Melanin poppin.
I see that glow you woke up to pray and slay.
You better let them know.

No Love

I had to distance myself from you.
I had to burn that bridge so yo weak ass couldn't
grasp to me.
Now watch this glow up from a distance baby.

God's Plan

I thought there was such a thing as
'finding myself'
as a whole and trouble will come no more.
Until trouble snuck through the back door.
God gave me the strength to fight trouble once more. In those trying
times,
I learned there wasn't such a thing as 'finding myself' as a whole.
I had to keep going through trying times just to keep trouble out my
home.
Things don't always go as planned.
God always help you find a part of yourself to help you win the battle
once again.

Note To Self

The truth may sound like you're wrong to those who can't withstand to what's right. At no point do you go back and forth on the truth.

Dope Soulz

Watching re-runs of our favorite shows and eating lemon pepper
wings.
You know what food does to me.
I love seeing your gap when you smile.
I never show mine, but I love the way you embrace yours.
Laying on your chest and sharing each other's goals.
I just love to see you at your best.

A Woman

I'm a woman of God.
A woman of peace.
A woman who's been hurt
before.
A woman still trying to mend
her heart.

Lovelace IV

Don't force anything.
If it's meant to be, the universe will make it happen.

My Pride and Joy

Chocolate Drop.
Nubian Queen.
You are so much more than what the eye can see.
If it comes to it, I don't mind laying my life down for you.
You're my sister. That's what a sister would do.
Flying overseas we had the whole plane to ourselves.
I stayed closed to you because I knew you were scared, and I was too.
With a bond that grows stronger with day, we're connected by the
heart.
Even though we're miles away,

Forever yours
Khloe.

Letter to Self

Dear Lovelace,

    I'm sorry I lost you....I just wanted you to feel loved.

I didn't think it would cost you a piece/peace of your soul and half of your heart. I hope you could learn to forgive me, and never hold this against me. I see you're more focused now and even though you were traumatized, you're not hopeless now. Even in your darkest days you drop down to your knees and thank God for the day. It's a good thing your mom taught you how to pray. Growing in so many ways I know you're gonna be fine. I just wish I could turn back the hands of time.

From : **T**

Know Yourself

Don't let their crazy words demolish your heart.
Don't believe them when they say you will only go so far.
They don't even know who you are.

Walk Away

Do you ever feel like he's doing the most but still no growth? Does he
give you a dozen of roses for every lost day?
Or does he come with a sunflower to bright up your day?
Is his phone always on 1% every dice game?
He had to drop the whole gang off, that's why he coming in late? You
smell the perfume again that's not familiar to yours?
You still haven't taken your friend's advice?
You know he cheats but he swears he gone make it right.
I'm not telling you what to do sweetheart,
but you know how to put the right foot before the left when you walk
away.

Peace Be With You

Lonely nights come with peace.
A smile from the sun comes with peace.
Have faith in what you believe, it will bring you peace.

Change in Faces

I could never look at you the same anymore.
I gave you a piece of me I don't want back anymore.

Reinvent Yourself

#1 Never play yourself and always have respect for yourself.

#2 If you love that man, do for that man but NEVER be a goofy for that man.

Gemini 3X

You were the right one that fixed my wrongs.
So how could you turn around and do me wrong?
I keep giving you the benefit of the doubt.
You were the one.
You flipped sides like a Gemini.
You were also the wrong one.

Out of love

They say you never know what you have until it's gone.
You knew exactly what you had.
You just wanted to see how strong my love could last.

Release

You're the only one that can get me out my element.
When all the pain you put me through builds up, I must release it.
Cutting up your shit always gave me a sense of releasement.
Keyed up your car just for the fuck of it. You remember all those
times you cheated for the fun of it?

Weakness

I paid close attention to what you said out of anger,
trying your hardest to break me down mentally,
and knowing my weakness was loving you.
After a while, I realized you were really scared of me. I was a
weakness of yours too.

No Evil

The eyes want what they can't SPEAK.
The mind wants what it can't HEAR.
The ears want what they can't SEE

Re-Birth

Letting go of any hope of you and me.
The shoulda, coulda, woulda.
At least I tried.
I'm feeling more beautiful and alive since God removed you from my side.

Lovelace V

They don't understand you.
So, they fear what they don't understand.

Self Service

Her: So, what are you bringing to the table?
Him: Not to be rude, but what are you bringing to the table?
Her: I am the table.

The Great Wall

I won't allow another person to hurt me. I will do everything in my power to protect my heart from being betrayed again. I built a wall stronger and taller than The Great Wall of China surrounding my heart. One day you approached my wall with so much grace and confidence. But that wasn't enough for me to let my guard down. I told you it's going to take more than an army to break my Great Wall down. You said, "I'm not here to break your wall down, leak myself through it, or climb over. Keep up the Great Wall. Let me gain your trust and loyalty from my side and when you're ready for me to give you the love that your heart deserves, I'll help you tear down The Great Wall."

Feel Her

I want you to hurt like you made her hurt.
I want you to spend a life sentence in her nightmare that you
implanted in her.
I hope you stare at broken clocks praying that time
heals your heart.

Black is ubiquitous

I see you carrying the world on your back, let me help you with that.
The most disrespected woman why would they do you like that?
How did they consign to oblivion that you were carrying
THEM ON YOUR BACK.
You're ubiquitous there is no life
without you.
She is me, I am her, and I won't forsake us.
I know your pain I stand with you, not against you.
As your sister I would hold this world with you.

Why Stay?

If it hurts so much why stay?
Why hold onto someone who's incapable to make you feel safe?
While they're the same person that's insisting you to stay.

Open up your
third eye.

Saturn Returns

It's a place of the unrevealed but I'm not scared.
A never-have before blessing, but I embrace it with open arms. I know
the universe will cause me no harm.
Floating in the rings of Saturn, for once the voices stopped whispering.
It's been a long time since I heard my heart singing.
This is the lifetime I've been waiting for. Shooting stars fly by,
no negatively has intervened my mind.
Intertwine with peace at this moment I know I'm where I'm
supposed to be.

River of Self-Forgiveness

Lost thoughts on purpose and found them for a purpose.
Kayaking down the river of self-forgiveness that led to the
ocean of
self-love.

I'm ready to get lost....you coming?

Never ending story

If the heart doesn't beat is there still love in there?
Would you still care for me?
Yes?
No?
Maybe so?
We'll see.
Like fairytales there's always a possible for infinity.

Sage Night

I'm losing my mind.
I'm becoming.
I'm growing.
I'm learning.
I'm just trying to stay in God's light.
In between a "perfect angel" and a "Devil's child"
I'm just like everyone else trying to end a war with myself and be at peace.

Lovelace VI

She wants to do right by God, but she loves street dudes.

4 Page Letter

It's been a long day, hours are ticking away and I'm yearning for a smile on my face. Sitting in the walk-in closet on the floor, I pulled out every letter you've ever written. Each letter feels like I'm reading it for the very first time. You talked about how you can't parallel park. I started laughing hysterically. It's true, I remember when you hit my car on Christmas Eve I was so mad at you. Three Tuesday night's death came to crush our hearts in those times our words to comfort each other's hearts. Your words of encouragement pushed me to pursue my dreams. I know you will forever be there for me. I don't expect anyone to understand as long as you know where my love stands.

Highly Favored

Smile in worries and
be grateful in troubles.
Be appreciative for the blessings you receive because they can be your
last of anything.

Lead the way

There is no path to peace.
It's something that comes alone with each step you take.
Not knowing your destination, just walking by
faith.

New Life.

Stop watering dead plants in hopes that one day it would rise again. It can be very difficult to let go of something you put your precious time toward. Don't invest your time and energy into something that won't give you life in return. It's alright to start fresh. Yes, it may take time for a new life to evolve but remember faith in God includes faith in God's timing.

The Pride Man

You always had a way of doing reverse psychology. Doing me wrong.
Then put the blame on me. Saying you're a real man, but that's not
what real men do.
You got too much pride to apologize, take accountability for your
actions, and just admit when you're in the wrong.

Bittersweet

You were my light.
You remember when we gave each other life?
Seeing you cry tears of joy when I gave you life.
I remember when I got comfort from your lies and how you brought
your dirty work to the light.

Lovelace VII

You're not right because you're not right with yourself.
Don't disrespect yourself again.

Superwoman

I was your psychiatrist, mother, chef, woman, and so forth.
You saw that I found happiness within myself. Not needing your
approval anymore, I moved on with my life for the better.
You said, "You're going to need me one day." What you failed to
realize, I built myself from the ground up with an indestructible
foundation of God's love. You can't get to me baby...remember you
needed me to be your
superwoman.

Self-Control

Never give someone the power to think you need them to survive.
Stand your ground baby.

Simple Things

I was mesmerized by how the waves kissed the rocks repeatedly, but you were mesmerized by me. You kissed my hand just how the waves kissed the rocks. You always had a way to make me feel like a queen. We both knew your singing is not the best, but I love the way you sang to me. With a smile that can light up so bright; just like the moon in the darkest night. You bring out the best in me with just the simplest thing in life.

More

I just want more of God and less of me.
Putting all my trust into the High Power to guide me in the right direction.

978 ∞

It's never the right time when time is never on your side

90's R&B

I wish we were still present like 90's R&B.
I never wanted to leave you in the past.

Epiphany

Holding the doorknob tight you want to let go, but your flesh is
procrastinating.
You feel your body rushing down a timeline reminiscing on the good
times.
The first day y'all met, thinking about soft kisses he placed on your
neck.
Within seconds, an epiphany can stop a rewind. Without question,
you walked out the door.
At that moment, you learned that love also can mean
letting go.

GPS

Him: Can I take you home? Where do you live?
Her: I live inside my head.

Don't Come Knocking

Times get hard, I wonder how I even got this far.
I hear a familiar knock at the door.
Check the peek hole, it's death knocking once more. I'm ignoring it this time. One day I have to open that door.
I'm not ready to throw the white flag in. I'm continuing to fight some more.

Different Type of Time

You sacrifice my emotions for a temporally feelings.
Now you want me to open the gates to heaven.
I accept bullshit in the past.
I won't accept that in the present.
This lifetime is made for love to last.

Lovelace VIII

I'm more than a snack or an entrée.
I'm priceless. I'm a
God.
I'm something that you can't imagine in your wildest dreams.

One on One

I will listen to everything that you tell me, and I won't question any
obstacle that comes my way. There may have been times I thought I
failed you, but you let me know I didn't fail you. I may have stumbled.
But my faith in you kept me going.

unlimited time

Without time there is no me
without time there is no you
without time there is no we
and without time there is no frequency

Mister Dream

I dream about you, but I don't know your name. Replaying scenarios but I can't see your face. I could feel your soft hands, and I could feel your love for me. You're in a place that no one dares to go. But I don't mind driving down that road.

Imperfections

Who said perfect means "perfect" anyways? Flaws and all, you're perfect for me.

Smoke God

You had a smile that could light up the sky.
You were there when I needed guidance through my dark times.
Who would've known a few days before would've been our last
goodbyes. I called you over 100 times. I wonder if I told you I loved
you over 100 times.
A cousin, friend it hurts my soul to know I can't be in your presence.
You always kept it 100 with me.
I pray you won't leave my memory.
Please?

Lost Time

You'd lose yourself trying to understand someone else.
It's not worth it.

Years In

Him: I'm ready I got my shit together I swear.
Her: I'm straight on you....I don't want you more (smiling)

Force

You cannot force trust but,
you can put your trust in the Lord.
You cannot force an apology, but you can pray for them.
Take what you're giving. Walk away and ask the Lord for healing.

From Mommy

When you see me, I pray you forgive me.
When the heaven's gate opens, I hope that you embrace me with
open arms.
I swear I meant you no harm.

Salut

The universe has been testing me displaying my feelings on a pedestal.
Knowing the facts can cut deep.
Just like a gloomy day, the dark clouds will drift away.
So, we salute to the pain with champagne.
This is just another rainy day.

Lovelace IX

Dead Memories – Memories that was once the greatest in the world.

One's Enemy

The same mind that kills you
is the same mind that heals you.
Infrequently you can be your own enemy.
Re-conceive dead memories that seize the best of you.

Speak into existence

Your mind is ready to unfold new feelings, a new scenery of life where there is an end, and there is a new beginning. Whatever bad energy that was clenched to your soul is no longer a part of you. Turning your weaknesses into your greatest strength. Fathom your mind to blessings. The real bag is a peace of mind.

Pronoia

(the belief that the universe is conspiring in your favor)

She was choosing me.
She was me.
She created a path to space leading me by the hand and take me away.
As I exist the earth's atmosphere a sensation of peace came over me.
My calling was me calling myself home.

Only for you

I'll break the rules for you...if you're willing to break them too.

Just Wondering

Do you remember the first time you were aware of life?
Or how the sky remains blue from morning to night?
Do you remember when you felt love at first sight?
Have you seen a bird learn how to fly on its own?
Do you ever wonder how the ocean waves can move without wind?
Or how you had your first kiss with someone who was more than just
a friend?
I'm just wondering

Patience

Don't lose respect for yourself just because you haven't met the right
man.
Feeling like you have to be a hoe just to get some attention.
Soul searching but really selling your soul.
Have morals lady.
Whatever's yours will come in due time.

BF

You bring joy into my life. Even when you're telling me right from wrong. Giving me the best advice and telling me the truth. Even if I don't want to hear it. We talk about our relationship problems and laugh all night. You're my best friend and my man. BF I swear I can't picture you out my life.

She

She just wants to travel the world.
She's not a gold digger.
She's unavailable to the unkind.
She's a GOAL digger.
She selfish with herself.
She's one of a kind.

Fear

I love you,
but I had a terrible fear that I'll become you.
I called you crying after that bad breakup. I felt just like you.
Was my worst nightmare coming true?
I had to keep all my faith in God. He was the only one that could pull me through.
I always knew that I'm much stronger than you; I just wished you found that strength that God gave you too.

Life, Love, Growth

Losing yourself is life.
Fighting for yourself is love.
Doing better for yourself is growth.

Hurricane

You always want peace in a storm that
you created.
We can't live in the eye of the storm forever baby.

Not Life

I had a dream of me and you.
Living the good life and me being your wife.
Then I woke up knowing that can't be
life.

Queen

Stand 10 toes down.
Never let them see you frown.
I know sometimes the pressure may be too much to bear.
Working 12 hours today but remaining strong. Not needing a man to depend on.
Stay independent my beautiful Queen. Never bow down to anyone or anything.

Lovelace X

You never gave up on what was most important and that was yourself.

Flower from concrete

I'm not who I thought I would be.
I've concluded maybe that wasn't made for me and I'm okay with
that. The better version of me is pushing through the cracks of the
concrete with one leaf at a time. Still delicate and divine.
I'm still in the process of growing gracefully and I'm getting better with
time.
I couldn't be more proud of me.

Good In Goodbye

I've never been a fan of goodbyes.
Consumed by wanderlust for good vibes.
Replacing bad energy with the stars in the sky.
Sorry, old friend, but this is the good in goodbye.

Relationships Goals

Self-love

½ of Me

God's decision was to only give me half of me and for me to ascertain the missing part he left for me. Who am I to force something that was already set in stone? It's a mystery to me, but he has already chosen my destiny.

Spoiled. Crazy. Selfish

You know I need the attention. I don't want to feel alone. You say it's time for you to hit the gym, then I beg for you to stay, because I need you near. You always give in when I do my sad puppy face. After that we both know you're not going anywhere.

Sweet Dreams

In the shower is when I think about you the most.
Remember, you were my man. I did anything for you.
When people were judging you, I didn't care. I thought we would grow old together.
After so long of feeding me sweet dreams, after a while, I started tasting lies.

Strong

You will never see me fold under pressure. I won't give you the satisfaction.

Who You Loyal To?

You talk about loyalty when you can't even be loyal to yourself.
You can't even be loyal to me.
Don't speak about loyalty if you don't know the meaning.

Big Mad

I'm a hoe because I don't feed into your bullshit anymore?
I'm a hoe just because I saw the light behind your dark soul?
Let me take a wild guess,
you're big mad because I'm not with you anymore.

Know It All

What up pretty lady?
Why you don't have a man by your side?
You must be a crazy lady?
Maybe dude hasn't been treating you right lately.
Let me fix it baby.
SHUT THE HELL UP
Who are you to fix some shit? You sound like an immature boy with that woopty woop.
That magic crystal ball won't do the trick.
Just because a woman is standing alone doesn't mean she can't hold her own.

10:12pm

When there are no words that can generate how you feel, all you think about is, "should I take these pills or just chill?" It takes a powerful person to defeat this will.

Fighting with the thoughts in my head. Can you please be still?

Broken Bond

She was the life of the party. It was unusual for her to miss a girl's night.

You received a phone call that changed your whole life. She died that very night.

At that moment it felt like you might as well take your own life.

She was your best friend. She knew you within and yall demons was the closest friends.

Fought like ying yang twins but it was nothing that could stop yall from being cool again.

It's like you and her was birth in the same womb. She always wanted to be under you, even though there was so much space in the room.

Now you're asking yourself what type of love this is? yall was supposed to die together and blow out the candles together.

Now you're alone and starting to feel this cold weather.

Your A1, day one, and right-hand man is gone.

How can better days come alone?

Déj've

26 years old but I've been here many moons before.

Survival

They killed half of your mind,
but never your soul.
You still got time to rebuild the other side.

Picture Perfect

Don't you think enough is enough?
You keep painting the same picture just with a different brush.
Your signature is on the side.
I'm just curious, did you think it would be hard to find? I see you.
I see the true colors that rose beneath you.

Forever is Never

My high is wearing off and you want me to stay longer?
The things we want to last forever....they never do.

Natural Beauty

Even at your worst, you're still at your best.

Blinded Enemy

So, you made me an enemy off your insecurities?
I have to remind myself you're young minded.
Investing your time and energy to know my next move.
You're blindsided. You will always lose.

Heart of Mino

They hear the bell ringing and they know I'm coming.
A force to be reckoned with. They know how I'm coming.
Know to never look my way.
Checking their energy if they got something to say.
I fight beside warrior queens.
Loyalty is the only thing we believe.
I am who they say I couldn't be.
A warrior of Mino I would fight to the last breath of me.

DO NOT DISTURB: ON

I want these guys to leave me alone.
At the same time, I feel so
alone.
If you can't bring me peace, don't call my phone

Thank You

You told me what I already know, but it's what I needed to hear.

Wrong turn, right time.

You made the wrong turn at the stop sign.
I told you to keep going. We still got more hours in this lifetime.

Rainbow Baby

It rains a lot in London, but your blessing came to clear that cloud
that rain on your parade. There's been times you questioned the man
above; your smile carries the pain.
You're learning to cope with the decision God's made.
Over the years you've found the good in goodbye and you give
without receiving.
You still love the unkind because you know everyone needs healing.
You found what was never lost, it was a piece/peace of yourself that
you buried and hope it got lost.

Keep moving forward

There is no such thing as a life without problems. We were born in a world of peaks and valleys. Now let that cry out, wipe your tears, and chase your dreams to the mountaintop.

It's You

Captivate by your determination to look within
me.
It was never a point in time you looked pasted me.

Assimilate

I had persuaded my own mind to think your heart was gold until pain change me.
Causing me to become my own mentor and the 1st lesson was to assimilate that everything that glitter isn't gold.

Saudade

We held each other up back to back and bone to bone.
When you left it felt like I was being forced to stand on my own.
A friendship that is one of a kind. I know it wasn't right for me to have a selfish mind.
We held each other tight and made an ocean with our tears when we had to say our goodbyes.
Every day I go back to the place where laughter was made, in hope it would give me serenity.
I wish you could return back, but the road you're on says no U-turn.

Goodnight

At night when you're holding me tight, I could feel your full lips on
my neck.
Giving me chills down my spine.
Feeling soul love by you.
Ending every night at peace with you.

Pain is love. Love is Pain

I know I can get on your nerves and I can be difficult, but I didn't
know you would put it down like that. Or that head on your shoulders
would love my body like that.

Underestimate

You didn't think I had the potential to succeed.
Well, look at me now. Don't sleep on awoke
woman.

Humble Down

When you're in a tough situation, always make good decision.
Don't let your circumstances define you.

Mo Lisa

Never bothered by the chaos coming her way, I called her Mo Lisa.
Because she is hiding a lot behind that gorgeous face.
Even after people betrayed her, nothing can take her glow away.
She takes the good and the bad. She knows it's a blessing anyway.
Never seeking revenge. Always search for peace within.
Mo Lisa will always have that beautiful smile on her face.

11:11

He said, " Make a wish baby the time is 11:11pm"

Temptation

You're that chocolate bar that I crave sometimes.
I always tell myself, "it's just this one last time."
Then I end up going back for more.
They say dark chocolate is good for you.
So why can't I have you all the time?

Maybe, Maybe Not

Perhaps we can smoke one in the future.
Ride around listen to music and joke around.
I know occasionally we agree to disagree.
We may have bad blood sometimes, but there is always chemistry.
If it's God's plan, possibly in the next lifetime, we can be lovers again.

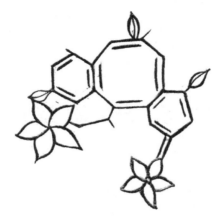

Wanderer

I've been thinking about the unthinkable again.

Voice Within

I need you to say this out loud.
"You're beautiful inside and out!"
Remember that voice inside your head can speak out loud too.
Inside is where you hind and contemplate everything, but that doesn't
mean love isn't within, that's where love begins. Sometimes you need
to let that voice speak out.
Be one with yourself.

World War III

Sometimes the flesh tries to overpower the spirit and questions God's actions. It's a constant battle between the two. Focus more on what you need and not what you want.

Violation of Self

When thinking too much your feelings can start to control your thoughts.
The mind can be a prison sometimes.
Challenge your inner-will power and set yourself free.

Lovelace XI

We all end on the wrong side of a love song in some point in a lifetime.

No U-turn

You stop choosing me to go after someone that's not even half of me. That doesn't even make sense to me. Maybe somethings are left to be unknown.
I'm someone's only choice now, don't even think about turning around.

Nodus Tollens

(The realization that the plot of your life doesn't make sense to you anymore)

It's like a slap in the face wanting to be in a place that won't bring me peace but is somewhat good for me.

I See You

Every beginning has an ending.

Aftermath

You want to switch up on me....go ahead be my guest. Don't start begging me when karma come next.

Overstimulated

She said, "Are you okay?"
I said, "Yes."
But deep down I'm a fucking mess.
My mind is racing at a pace I can't understand.
Here we go with this shit again.

1st

Focusing on my growth and choosing myself will always come 1st.
It's nothing personal.
I didn't change. I just found myself.

Cloud 9

I want you to be in me like the blood in my veins.
I want to feel your tongue running access my pain.
Can we make love in the rain?

Small Getaway

Me being in your head was just a place for me to getaway.

24 Hours

3 hours has passed. Not a single word has come out of my mouth.
That voice that's lingering around is the only thing I think about.
Wanting to desire me more,
stop feeling pity for myself, and to know God has so much in store.
Knowing dark days and having the patience for the moonlight,
I just want to be a better me before sunrise.

Faith

Speak your blessing into existence and never let it exist your mind. Never lose hope for what you seek for, even when going through tough times.

Lovelace XII

Reach inside your soul and give yourself a hug.

Another Level

When they mistake your kindness for a flaw,
remain humble,
they weren't built like you.

Your Calling

You can hind from the outside world.
But you can't hind from yourself.
Remember a situation is only temporary. Never make it your
destination.

Nothing More, Nothing Less

I only wanted to share the drugs and music with you. I'm sorry, I can't be more then that with you.

Self-inflict

Closing that chapter with you taught me to love myself so much more.
All the love I install into you was given to another with no hesitation,
not a blink of the eye, or no consideration.
I will never inflict self-harm with being pressed over you again.

Change is Inevitable

My way of thinking is constantly
changing.
I'm seeing things for what it really is,
not for what it could be, or what I want it to be.
I don't feel like the same person I was a month ago.
I wonder if that's not me anymore.

God's Child II

You want a love like your own until you recognize it's okay to be alone, so you adore yourself more. On a quest to get to the glorious part of yourself, you're embracing this freedom.

Bra off, hair down and your skin is clearing up now.

A. Peace
of
Lovelace